2

BACK RIDGE

Work only in loops indicated by arrows *(Fig. 1)*.

Fig. 1

FREE LOOPS OF A CHAIN

When instructed to work in free loops of a chain, work in loop indicated by arrow *(Fig. 2)*.

Fig. 2

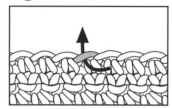

FRINGE

Cut a piece of cardboard 3" (7.5 cm) wide and 6¹/₂" (16.5 mm) long. Wind the yarn **loosely** and **evenly** lengthwise around the cardboard until the card is filled, then cut across one end; repeat as needed.

Hold together as many strands as specified in individual instructions; fold in half.

With **wrong** side facing and using a crochet hook, draw the folded end up through a stitch or space and pull the loose ends through the folded end *(Fig. 3a)*; draw the knot up **tightly** *(Fig. 3b)*. Repeat, spacing as specified in individual instructions.

Lay flat on a hard surface and trim the ends.

Fig. 3a

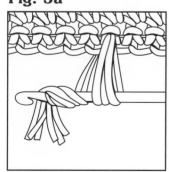

Fig. 3b

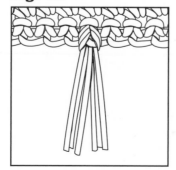

1. TWINKLES

Shown on Back Cover.

Finished Size: 34¹/₂" x 46" (87.5 cm x 117 cm)

MATERIALS

Bulky Weight Yarn:
31¹/₂ ounces, 770 yards
(890 grams, 704 meters)
Crochet hook, size N (9 mm) **or** size needed for gauge

GAUGE: In pattern, (sc, ch 1) 4 times = 4" (10 cm); 9 rows = 5" (12.75 cm)

Gauge Swatch: 4¹/₂"w x 5"h
(11.5 cm x 12.75 cm)
Ch 10.
Work same as Afghan for 9 rows.
Finish off.

AFGHAN

Ch 70.

Row 1 (Right side)**:** Sc in second ch from hook, ★ ch 1, skip next ch, sc in next ch; repeat from ★ across: 35 sc and 34 ch-1 sps.

Note: Loop a short piece of yarn around any stitch to mark Row 1 as **right** side.

Row 2: Ch 1, turn; sc in first sc and in next ch-1 sp, (ch 1, sc in next ch-1 sp) across to last sc, sc in last sc: 36 sc and 33 ch-1 sps.

Row 3: Ch 1, turn; sc in first sc, ch 1, (sc in next ch-1 sp, ch 1) across to last 2 sc, skip next sc, sc in last sc: 35 sc and 34 ch-1 sps.

Repeat Rows 2 and 3 for pattern until Afghan measures approximately 46" (117 cm) from beginning ch, ending by working Row 3.

Finish off.

Holding 4 strands of yarn together, add fringe in sps across short edges of Afghan *(Figs. 3a & b)*.

2. STARGAZER

Shown on page 2.

Finished Size: 36$\frac{1}{2}$" x 46" (92.5 cm x 117 cm)

MATERIALS
Bulky Weight Yarn:
   Blue - 20 ounces, 495 yards
     (570 grams, 452.5 meters)
   Pink - 14 ounces, 345 yards
     (400 grams, 315.5 meters)
   Crochet hook, size N (9 mm) **or** size needed
    for gauge

GAUGE: In pattern, one repeat
        (sc, 5-dc group) = 3" (7.5 cm);
        4 rows = 3$\frac{1}{4}$" (8.25 cm)

Gauge Swatch: 6$\frac{1}{2}$"w x 3$\frac{1}{4}$"h
           (16.5 cm x 8.25 cm)
With Blue, ch 14.
Work same as Afghan for 4 rows.
Finish off.

AFGHAN
With Blue, ch 74.

Row 1 (Right side)**:** Working in back ridges of beginning ch *(Fig. 1, page 3)*, sc in second ch from hook, ★ skip next 2 chs, 5 dc in next ch, skip next 2 chs, sc in next ch; repeat from ★ across; finish off: 73 sts.

Note: Loop a short piece of yarn around any stitch to mark Row 1 as **right** side.

Row 2: With **wrong** side facing, join Pink with dc in first sc *(see Joining With Dc, page 1)*; dc in same st, ch 1, skip next 2 dc, sc in next dc, ch 1, ★ skip next 2 dc, (dc, ch 1) twice in next sc, skip next 2 dc, sc in next dc, ch 1; repeat from ★ across to last 3 sts, skip next 2 dc, 2 dc in last sc: 38 sts and 35 ch-1 sps.

Row 3: Ch 3 **(counts as first dc, now and throughout)**, turn; 2 dc in same st, skip next ch-1 sp, sc in next sc, skip next ch-1 sp, ★ 5 dc in next ch-1 sp, skip next ch-1 sp, sc in next sc, skip next ch-1 sp; repeat from ★ across to last 2 dc, skip next dc, 3 dc in last dc; finish off: 73 sts.

Row 4: With **wrong** side facing, join Blue with sc in first dc *(see Joining With Sc, page 1)*; ★ ch 1, skip next 2 dc, (dc, ch 1) twice in next sc, skip next 2 dc, sc in next dc; repeat from ★ across: 37 sts and 36 ch-1 sps.

Row 5: Ch 1, turn; sc in first sc, ★ skip next ch-1 sp, 5 dc in next ch-1 sp, skip next ch-1 sp, sc in next sc; repeat from ★ across; finish off: 73 sts.

Row 6: With **wrong** side facing, join Pink with dc in first sc; dc in same st, ch 1, skip next 2 dc, sc in next dc, ch 1, ★ skip next 2 dc, (dc, ch 1) twice in next sc, skip next 2 dc, sc in next dc, ch 1; repeat from ★ across to last 3 sts, skip next 2 dc, 2 dc in last sc: 38 sts and 35 ch-1 sps.

Row 7: Ch 3, turn; 2 dc in same st, skip next ch-1 sp, sc in next sc, skip next ch-1 sp, ★ 5 dc in next ch-1 sp, skip next ch-1 sp, sc in next sc, skip next ch-1 sp; repeat from ★ across to last 2 dc, skip next dc, 3 dc in last dc; finish off: 73 sts.

Row 8: With **wrong** side facing, join Blue with sc in first dc; ★ ch 1, skip next 2 dc, (dc, ch 1) twice in next sc, skip next 2 dc, sc in next dc; repeat from ★ across: 37 sts and 36 ch-1 sps.

Rows 9-56: Repeat Rows 5-8, 12 times.

Finish off.

Holding 6 strands of Blue together, add fringe evenly spaced across short edges of Afghan *(Figs. 3a & b, page 3)*.

4

3

5

4

3. SWEET DREAMS

Shown on page 5.

Finished Size: 36¹/₂" x 49"
                   (92.5 cm x 124.5 cm)

MATERIALS
Bulky Weight Yarn:
   White - 15 ounces, 370 yards
      (430 grams, 338.5 meters)
   Pink - 9¹/₂ ounces, 235 yards
      (270 grams, 215 meters)
   Variegated - 9 ounces, 220 yards
      (260 grams, 201 meters)
Crochet hook, size N (9 mm) **or** size needed
   for gauge

GAUGE: In pattern, 8 dc = 5" (12.75 cm);
           9 rows = 8" (20.25 cm)

Gauge Swatch: 5"w x 4"h (12.75 cm x 10 cm)
With Pink, ch 11.
Work same as Afghan Body for 4 rows.
Finish off.

AFGHAN BODY
With Pink, ch 59, place marker in third ch from
hook for st placement.

Row 1 (Right side)**:** 2 Dc in fifth ch from hook,
(skip next ch, 2 dc in next ch) across to last 2 chs,
skip next ch, dc in last ch; finish off: 55 dc.

Note: Loop a short piece of yarn around any
stitch to mark Row 1 as **right** side.

Row 2: With **wrong** side facing, join Variegated
with dc in first dc *(see Joining With Dc,
page 1)*; skip next dc, 2 dc in sp **before** next dc
(Fig. 4), (skip next 2 dc, 2 dc in sp **before** next
dc) across to last dc, skip last dc, dc in next ch;
finish off: 56 dc.

Fig. 4

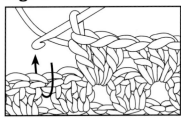

Row 3: With **right** side facing, join Pink with dc
in first dc; skip next dc, 2 dc in sp **before** next dc,
(skip next 2 dc, 2 dc in sp **before** next dc) across
to last 2 dc, skip next dc, dc in last dc; finish off.

Row 4: With **wrong** side facing, join White with
dc in first dc; skip next dc, 2 dc in sp **before** next
dc, (skip next 2 dc, 2 dc in sp **before** next dc)
across to last 2 dc, skip next dc, dc in last dc; do
not finish off.

Row 5: Ch 3 **(counts as first dc, now and
throughout)**, turn; skip next dc, 2 dc in sp
before next dc, (skip next 2 dc, 2 dc in sp **before**
next dc) across to last 2 dc, skip next dc, dc in last
dc; finish off.

Row 6: With **wrong** side facing, join Variegated
with dc in first dc; skip next dc, 2 dc in sp **before**
next dc, (skip next 2 dc, 2 dc in sp **before** next
dc) across to last 2 dc, skip next dc, dc in last dc;
finish off.

Row 7: With **right** side facing, join Pink with dc
in first dc; skip next dc, 2 dc in sp **before** next dc,
(skip next 2 dc, 2 dc in sp **before** next dc) across
to last 2 dc, skip next dc, dc in last dc; finish off.

Row 8: With **wrong** side facing, join Variegated
with dc in first dc; skip next dc, 2 dc in sp **before**
next dc, (skip next 2 dc, 2 dc in sp **before** next
dc) across to last 2 dc, skip next dc, dc in last dc;
finish off.

Row 9: With **right** side facing, join White with dc
in first dc; skip next dc, 2 dc in sp **before** next dc,
(skip next 2 dc, 2 dc in sp **before** next dc) across
to last 2 dc, skip next dc, dc in last dc; do **not**
finish off.

Row 10: Ch 3, turn; skip next dc, 2 dc in sp
before next dc, (skip next 2 dc, 2 dc in sp **before**
next dc) across to last 2 dc, skip next dc, dc in last
dc; finish off.

Row 11: With **right** side facing, join Pink with dc
in first dc; skip next dc, 2 dc in sp **before** next dc,
(skip next 2 dc, 2 dc in sp **before** next dc) across
to last 2 dc, skip next dc, dc in last dc; finish off.

Row 12: With **wrong** side facing, join Variegated
with dc in first dc; skip next dc, 2 dc in sp **before**
next dc, (skip next 2 dc, 2 dc in sp **before** next
dc) across to last 2 dc, skip next dc, dc in last dc;
finish off.

Rows 13-53: Repeat Rows 3-12, 4 times; then
repeat Row 3 once **more**.

EDGING

Rnd 1: With **right** side facing, join White with sc in first dc on Row 53 *(see Joining With Sc, page 1)*; sc in same st and in each dc across to last dc, 3 sc in last dc; sc evenly across end of rows; working in free loops of beginning ch *(Fig. 2, page 3)*, 3 sc in first ch, sc in each ch across to marked ch, 3 sc in marked ch; sc evenly across end of rows, sc in same st as first sc; join with slip st to first sc.

Rnd 2: Ch 1, 3 sc in same st, sc in each sc around working 3 sc in center sc of each corner 3-sc group; join with slip st to first sc, finish off.

---

4. ANGEL BLUSH

Shown on page 6.

Finished Size: 36" x 46" (91.5 cm x 117 cm)

MATERIALS
Bulky Weight Yarn:
    White - 17 ounces, 420 yards
      (480 grams, 384 meters)
    Pink - 14$\frac{1}{2}$ ounces, 360 yards
      (410 grams, 329 meters)
    Crochet hook, size N (9 mm) **or** size needed
      for gauge

GAUGE: In pattern, from point to point
          (16 sts) = 7$\frac{1}{4}$" (18.5 cm);
          4 rows = 5" (12.75 cm)

Gauge Swatch: 4" (10 cm) square
With White, ch 8.
Row 1: Sc in second ch from hook and in each ch across: 7 sc.
Rows 2-8: Ch 1, turn; sc in each sc across. Finish off.

STITCH GUIDE

DECREASE (uses next 3 sts)
★ YO, insert hook in **next** st, YO and pull up a loop, YO and draw through 2 loops on hook; repeat from ★ 2 times **more**, YO and draw through all 4 loops on hook **(counts as one dc)**.

AFGHAN
With White, ch 83.

Row 1 (Right side): Working in back ridges of beginning ch *(Fig. 1, page 3)*, 2 dc in fourth ch from hook **(3 skipped chs count as first dc)**, dc in next 4 chs, decrease twice, dc in next 4 chs, ★ 3 dc in each of next 2 chs, dc in next 4 chs, decrease twice, dc in next 4 chs; repeat from ★ across to last ch, 3 dc in last ch; finish off: 80 dc.

Note: Loop a short piece of yarn around any stitch to mark Row 1 as **right** side.

Row 2: With **wrong** side facing, join Pink with dc in first dc *(see Joining With Dc, page 1)*; 2 dc in same st, dc in next 4 dc, decrease twice, dc in next 4 dc, ★ 3 dc in each of next 2 dc, dc in next 4 dc, decrease twice, dc in next 4 dc; repeat from ★ across to last dc, 3 dc in last dc; finish off.

Row 3: With **right** side facing, join White with dc in first dc; 2 dc in same st, dc in next 4 dc, decrease twice, dc in next 4 dc, ★ 3 dc in each of next 2 dc, dc in next 4 dc, decrease twice, dc in next 4 dc; repeat from ★ across to last dc, 3 dc in last dc; finish off.

Row 4: With **wrong** side facing, join Pink with dc in first dc; 2 dc in same st, dc in next 4 dc, decrease twice, dc in next 4 dc, ★ 3 dc in each of next 2 dc, dc in next 4 dc, decrease twice, dc in next 4 dc; repeat from ★ across to last dc, 3 dc in last dc; finish off.

Repeat Rows 3 and 4 for pattern until Afghan measures approximately 46" (117 cm) from beginning ch, ending by working Row 3.

7

5

5. HUGGLES

Shown on page 10.

Finished Size: 35" x 47" (89 cm x 119.5 cm)

MATERIALS
Bulky Weight Yarn:
    White - 18 ounces, 445 yards
        (510 grams, 407 meters)
    Blue - 9 ounces, 220 yards
        (260 grams, 201 meters)
    Pink - 9 ounces, 220 yards
        (260 grams, 201 meters)
    Crochet hook, size N (9 mm) **or** size needed
        for gauge

GAUGE: In pattern, 8 sts = 4¹/₂" (11.5 cm);
          6 rows = 5" (12.75 cm)

Gauge Swatch: 4¹/₂"w x 5"h
                (11.5 cm x 12.75 cm)
With White, ch 9.
Row 1: Sc in second ch from hook and in each
sc across: 7 sc.
Row 2: Ch 3 **(counts as first dc)**, turn; dc in
next sc and in each sc across.
Row 3: Ch 1, turn; sc in each dc across.
Rows 4-6: Repeat Rows 2 and 3 once, then
repeat Row 2 once **more**.
Finish off.

AFGHAN BODY
With White, ch 61.

Row 1 (Right side)**:** Sc in second ch from hook
and in next 3 chs changing to Blue in last sc
(Fig. 5a), sc in next 4 chs changing to White in
last sc, ★ sc in next 4 chs changing to Blue in last
sc, sc in next 4 chs changing to White in last sc;
repeat from ★ across to last 4 chs, sc in last 4 chs:
60 sc.

Note: Loop a short piece of yarn around any
stitch to mark Row 1 as **right** side.

Row 2: Ch 3 **(counts as first dc, now and
throughout)**, turn; dc in next 3 sc changing to
Blue in last dc *(Fig. 5b)*, dc in next 4 sc changing
to White in last dc, ★ dc in next 4 sc changing to
Blue in last dc, dc in next 4 sc changing to White
in last dc; repeat from ★ across to last 4 sc, dc in
last 4 sc changing to Pink in last dc.

Continue changing colors in same manner.

Row 3: With Pink ch 1, turn; sc in first 4 dc,
(with White sc in next 4 dc, with Pink sc in next
4 dc) across.

Row 4: Ch 3, turn; dc in next 3 sc, (with White
dc in next 4 sc, with Pink dc in next 4 sc) across.

Row 5: With White ch 1, turn; sc in first 4 dc,
(with Blue sc in next 4 dc, with White sc in next
4 dc) across.

Row 6: Ch 3, turn; dc in next 3 sc, (with Blue dc
in next 4 sc, with White dc in next 4 sc) across.

Rows 7-54: Repeat Rows 3-6, 12 times; at end
of Row 54, cut Blue and Pink.

EDGING
Rnd 1: With White ch 1, turn; 2 sc in first dc, sc
in each dc across to last dc, 3 sc in last dc; sc
evenly across end of rows; working in free loops of
beginning ch *(Fig. 2, page 3)*, 3 sc in first ch, sc
in each ch across to ch at base of last sc, 3 sc in
next ch; sc evenly across end of rows, sc in same
st as first sc; join with slip st to first sc.

Rnd 2: Ch 1, do **not** turn; 3 sc in same st, sc in
each sc around working 3 sc in center sc of each
corner 3-sc group; join with slip st to first sc,
finish off.

CHANGING COLORS
Work the last stitch to within one step of
completion, hook new yarn *(Fig. 5a or 5b)* and
draw through both loops on hook. Do not cut old
color. Work over color not being used, holding it
with normal tension across top of previous row.

Fig. 5a

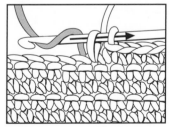

Fig. 5b

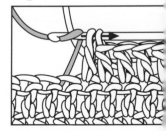

11

6. SLEEPY-BYE

Shown on Front Cover.

Finished Size: 34" x 45½" (86.5 cm x 115.5 cm)

MATERIALS
Bulky Weight Yarn:
    White - 12½ ounces, 310 yards
      (360 grams, 283.5 meters)
    Blue - 11 ounces, 270 yards
      (310 grams, 247 meters)
    Lt Blue - 10½ ounces, 260 yards
      (300 grams, 237.5 meters)
Crochet hook, size N (9 mm) **or** size needed
    for gauge

GAUGE: In pattern,
       7 sts and 8 rows = 4" (10 cm)

Gauge Swatch: 4" (10 cm) square
With Blue, ch 8.
Row 1: Sc in second ch from hook and in each ch across: 7 sc.
Rows 2-8: Ch 1, turn; sc in each sc across.
Finish off.

STITCH GUIDE

LONG DOUBLE CROCHET
(abbreviated LDC)
YO, working **around** chs of last 2 rows *(Fig. 6)*, insert hook in st indicated, YO and pull up a loop even with last st made (3 loops on hook), (YO and draw through 2 loops on hook) twice.

Fig. 6

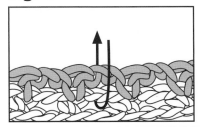

AFGHAN BODY
With Lt Blue, ch 58.

Row 1 (Right side)**:** Sc in second ch from hook and in next 3 chs, ch 1, ★ skip next ch, sc in next 5 chs, ch 1; repeat from ★ across to last 5 chs, skip next ch, sc in last 4 chs: 48 sc and 9 ch-1 sps.

Note: Loop a short piece of yarn around any stitch to mark Row 1 as **right** side.

Row 2: Ch 1, turn; sc in first 4 sc, ch 1, (sc in next 5 sc, ch 1) across to last 4 sc, sc in last 4 sc; finish off.

Row 3: With **right** side facing, join Blue with sc in first sc *(see Joining With Sc, page 1)*; ch 1, ★ skip next sc, sc in next 2 sc, work LDC in skipped beginning ch **below** next ch, sc in next 2 sc on Row 2, ch 1; repeat from ★ across to last 2 sc, skip next sc, sc in last sc: 47 sts and 10 ch-1 sps.

Row 4: Ch 1, turn; sc in first sc, ch 1, ★ skip next ch, sc in next 5 sts, ch 1; repeat from ★ across to last 2 sts, skip next ch, sc in last sc; finish off.

Row 5: With **right** side facing, join White with sc in first sc; work LDC in skipped sc 2 rows **below** next ch, ★ sc in next 2 sc on previous row, ch 1, skip next sc, sc in next 2 sc, work LDC in skipped sc 2 rows **below** next ch; repeat from ★ across to last sc on previous row, sc in last sc: 48 sts and 9 ch-1 sps.

Row 6: Ch 1, turn; sc in first 4 sts, ch 1, ★ skip next ch, sc in next 5 sts, ch 1; repeat from ★ across to last 5 sts, skip next ch, sc in last 4 sts; finish off.

Row 7: With **right** side facing, join Lt Blue with sc in first sc; ch 1, ★ skip next sc, sc in next 2 sc, work LDC in skipped sc 2 rows **below** next ch, sc in next 2 sc on previous row, ch 1; repeat from ★ across to last 2 sc, skip next sc, sc in last sc: 47 sts and 10 ch-1 sps.

Row 8: Ch 1, turn; sc in first sc, ch 1, ★ skip next ch, sc in next 5 sts, ch 1; repeat from ★ across to last 2 sts, skip next ch, sc in last sc; finish off.

Continued on page 13.

Row 9: With **right** side facing, join Blue with sc in first sc; work LDC in skipped sc 2 rows **below** next ch, ★ sc in next 2 sc on previous row, ch 1, skip next sc, sc in next 2 sc, work LDC in skipped sc 2 rows **below** next ch; repeat from ★ across to last sc on previous row, sc in last sc: 48 sts and 9 ch-1 sps.

Row 10: Ch 1, turn; sc in first 4 sts, ch 1, ★ skip next ch, sc in next 5 sts, ch 1; repeat from ★ across to last 5 sts, skip next ch, sc in last 4 sts; finish off.

Row 11: With **right** side facing, join White with sc in first sc; ch 1, ★ skip next sc, sc in next 2 sc, work LDC in skipped sc 2 rows **below** next ch, sc in next 2 sc on previous row, ch 1; repeat from ★ across to last 2 sc, skip next sc, sc in last sc: 47 sts and 10 ch-1 sps.

Row 12: Ch 1, turn; sc in first sc, ch 1, ★ skip next ch, sc in next 5 sts, ch 1; repeat from ★ across to last 2 sts, skip next ch, sc in last sc; finish off.

Row 13: With **right** side facing, join Lt Blue with sc in first sc; work LDC in skipped sc 2 rows **below** next ch, ★ sc in next 2 sc on previous row, ch 1, skip next sc, sc in next 2 sc, work LDC in skipped sc 2 rows **below** next ch; repeat from ★ across to last sc on previous row, sc in last sc: 48 sts and 9 ch-1 sps.

Row 14: Ch 1, turn; sc in first 4 sts, ch 1, ★ skip next ch, sc in next 5 sts, ch 1; repeat from ★ across to last 5 sts, skip next ch, sc in last 4 sts; finish off.

Row 15: With **right** side facing, join Blue with sc in first sc; ch 1, ★ skip next sc, sc in next 2 sc, work LDC in skipped sc 2 rows **below** next ch, sc in next 2 sc on previous row, ch 1; repeat from ★ across to last 2 sc, skip next sc, sc in last sc: 47 sts and 10 ch-1 sps.

Rows 16-87: Repeat Rows 4-15, 6 times.

Row 88: Ch 1, turn; sc in first sc and in each ch-1 sp and each st across; finish off: 57 sc.

EDGING
Rnd 1: With **right** side facing, join White with sc in first sc on Row 88; sc in same st and in each st across to last sc, 3 sc in last sc; sc evenly across end of rows; working in free loops of beginning ch *(Fig. 2, page 3)*, 3 sc in first ch, sc in each ch across to ch at base of last sc, 3 sc in next ch; sc evenly across end of rows, sc in same st as first sc join with slip st to first sc.

Rnd 2: Ch 1, 3 sc in same st, sc in each sc around working 3 sc in center sc of each corner 3-sc group; join with slip st to first sc, finish off.

---

7. MOON BEAM

Shown on page 9.

Finished Size: 35" x 46" (89 cm x 117 cm)

MATERIALS
Bulky Weight Yarn:
  Blue - 17$\frac{1}{2}$ ounces, 430 yards
    (500 grams, 393 meters)
  White - 13 ounces, 320 yards
    (370 grams, 292.5 meters)
Crochet hook, size N (9 mm) **or** size needed for gauge

GAUGE: In pattern, 7 sts and
          6 rows = 4" (10 cm)

Gauge Swatch: 4"w x 4$\frac{1}{2}$"h (10 cm x 11.5 cm)
With Blue, ch 8.
Work same as Afghan through Row 7.
Finish off.

AFGHAN
With Blue, ch 62.

Row 1 (Right side)**:** Sc in second ch from hook and in each ch across: 61 sc.

Note: Loop a short piece of yarn around any stitch to mark Row 1 as **right** side.

Row 2: Ch 3 **(counts as first dc, now and throughout)**, turn; dc in next sc and in each sc across.